Treasures Beneath the Sea

by ROBERT SILVERBERG

Illustrated by Mort Kunstler

SCHOLASTIC BOOK SERVICES

NEW YORK · TORONTO · LONDON · AUCKLAND · SYDNEY

This book is sold subject to the condition that it shall not be resold, lent, or otherwise circulated in any binding or cover other than that in which it is published — unless prior written permission has been obtained from the publisher — and without a similar condition, including this condition, being imposed on the subsequent purchaser.

Text copyright © 1960 by Western Publishing Company, Inc. Illustrations copyright © 1971 by Scholastic Magazines, Inc. This edition is published by Scholastic Book Services, a division of Scholastic Magazines, Inc., by arrangement with Western Publishing Company, Inc.

1st printing .... November 1971

Printed in the U.S.A.

Contents

Greenland

North
America

Hell Gate

Bay of Biscay
Vigo Bay

N

Caribbean
Sea

South
America

Europe

Asia

Africa

Manila Bay

Australia

New Zealand

Treasures Beneath
the Sea

Beneath the Sea

*

TREASURE, wonderful treasure, lies far below the troubled surface of the sea. It is treasure greater than all the vaults of Fort Knox could contain, and it rests, unguarded, on the ocean floor.

One eighth of all the gold and silver mined since the sixteenth century is down there. Rubies and gleaming emeralds, gold and silver coins, gold taken from the earth of Peru by sweating Inca slaves, diamonds and pearls — all lie in the ocean's tight grasp. Down below, in the rotting timbers of the ships of the past, lies wealth beyond belief.

Time and again men have gone into the dark depths in hopes of bringing back these lost riches. Lives have been lost, fortunes spent without result — and other fortunes have been won by lucky treasure hunters. This is the story of the treasure beneath the sea, and of the men whose boldness brought them sometimes wealth, sometimes heartbreak.

The Silver of Spain

"GIVE ME A SHIP, your Majesty," towering young William Phips pleaded. "Give me a ship and I'll fill your Majesty's treasury with Spanish silver!"

It was the year 1683. Easy-going, free-spending Charles II was on the English throne. The giant American, William Phips, had come to Charles with an idea. If the king would grant him a ship, Phips would search for sunken treasure in the West Indies. He would give the king a share of all he found.

"You may have the ship," the king declared. "But one fourth of the treasure will be mine!"

William Phips could not argue. He had nothing but his boldness and his great strength. The king had ships to spare. And so it was agreed: one fourth of the treasure would be the king's.

Phips was thirty-two. He had been born in the Maine woods, the twenty-first son of a rugged pioneer. At eighteen, young Phips went to Boston as a helper to a ship's carpenter. He learned about the sea there, and heard about sunken treasure too. Once a fortuneteller told him, "When you are thirty-seven you will find a great treasure. When you are forty-one the king will employ you in a great trust beyond the sea."

Bill Phips had dreamed of hunting treasure from that day on. He went to England and there he met the Duke of Albemarle, who had introduced Phips to King Charles. And now the king had given him a ship.

Phips set sail in the eighteen-gun frigate, *The Algier Rose*. He had a crew of ninety-five men. Instead of

wages, the men would receive shares in any treasure that was found.

The treasure Phips was looking for had gone down in 1643. Sixteen Spanish ships called galleons had been bound for Spain with silver and gold from the New World. As they headed toward the open sea, a storm struck. The helpless treasure fleet was driven toward a group of tiny islands and coral reefs known as the Abroxes.

The sea boiled up in foam over the dangerous rocks. Wise captains steered clear of the "Boilers," as they were called. But the wind drove the Spanish galleons right onto the reefs. Their hulls were shattered and they sank.

One ship, the vice-admiral's flagship, was swept clear across the reef and its side was smashed open. It went down between two rocks. One of the rocks stuck out of the water like a gravestone marking the spot.

Only two of the sixteen ships reached Spain to tell the tale. Millions of dollars of treasure lay under the waves.

Many adventurers tried to find the lost hoard. Some of it was found. But not the greatest treasure of all, that of the vice-admiral's flagship.

Finding it was William Phips' great dream.

The Algier Rose sailed first to Boston. The crew had a riotous time there, and everyone nearly ended in jail. Only when Phips told the governor he was on the king's business were they freed. It was a rough crew, but Phips was strong and rough himself, and he could handle them.

They sailed south toward the West Indies. But Phips' treasure map turned out to be worthless. They could not find the wreck. Up and down the sea they cruised. The discouraged crew urged Phips to forget about the sunken treasure and turn pirate. He refused. They attacked him, but he cut down the ringleader and quieted the rest at gun point. Then he landed in Jamaica and put all but a few of his unruly crew ashore.

Signing up a new crew, the brave captain headed for the Abroxes, still looking for the tall rock that marked the treasure ship's grave. Months passed. The ship was

leaky and food was low. There was nothing to do but return to England empty-handed.

By now King Charles was dead and James II was on the throne. Captain Phips begged the new king for a second chance.

King James gave Phips permission to seek the treasure again. Only this time he would have to supply his own ship. The king would give nothing but a license to search. For this he demanded a tenth of the profits.

Phips organized a group called the Gentleman Adventurers who paid for his new expedition. With their backing he bought two ships: the *James and Mary* and the *Henry of London.*

Once again he sailed for the New World.

The two ships anchored near the island of Hispaniola, which today is divided into Haiti and the Dominican Republic. This was where the Spanish galleons had started from, forty-three years before. In January, 1687, Phips sent the *Henry* off to the Abroxes reefs to look around.

The ship was gone three weeks. Storms raged in the region. Finally she came back, and Phips' heart sank when he saw the sad faces of her crew. The weather had allowed them only two or three days to explore, they said unhappily. They had found nothing.

"God will help us," Phips said solemnly. "We must be patient and keep on trying."

But then the men of the *Henry* began to laugh. They told their captain they had played a trick on him. Before his astonished eyes they produced a huge bar of silver coated with coral. They showed bars, coins, thousands of dollars of treasure! They *had* found the sunken ship!

Excitedly they now told him the true story of their trip. They had sailed northward to the dreaded Boilers, but nowhere did they find the tall, jutting rock that was said to mark the treasure ship. They searched back and forth over the reefs. Four Indian divers went down again and again. But the "ships" they saw in the water always turned out to be only big rocks.

The Indian divers could hold their breath for two minutes at a time. They went down forty, fifty, sixty feet. But they found nothing. They were attacked by vicious eels and threatened by sharks. It was exhausting, dangerous work.

On the second day Franko, one of the divers, was forty feet under the surface. He saw a lovely piece of red coral. He reached out to take it as a souvenir. Then he jerked on his line and came quickly to the surface. His eyes were big with amazement.

"Guns!" he cried. "I saw guns down there!"

The other divers went down at once. One came up with an odd-shaped coral lump that turned out to be a silver ingot. The explorers were right over the sunken treasure ship!

But where was the jutting rock? Everyone knew that such a rock had marked the lost ship's position.

The mystery was soon solved. The rock had been soft. In forty-three years the waves had worn it down. Its stump remained, below the surface. At its base lay the shattered treasure ship. Coral and seaweed had grown over everything, hiding it. Only a wild stroke of luck had led the diver to it.

The divers picked up eighty-two bars of silver and two thousand coins called pieces of eight. Then the weather turned bad, so the men of the *Henry* had returned to Hispaniola.

Several weeks later both ships sailed out. In five days they were at the Ambrosia Bank of the reef, where the treasure lay. They dropped anchor. That evening two divers went down and found eighty-nine pieces of eight. The adventurers gloated happily over the big silver coins.

Now the diving began in earnest. The four Indians dived repeatedly. They carried big stones under their arms to weigh them down. When they reached bottom, they dropped the stones and pulled bars of treasure free. Ropes drew them to the surface when the divers signaled.

For several days they worked very hard. The hold of the *James and Mary* filled rapidly with heavy Spanish coins. On Sunday they rested and Captain Phips led his men in a thanksgiving ceremony.

The next day Phips received troubling news. Two

sails had been spied to windward. Could pirates, who roamed the seas then, be coming to rob the treasure hunters, Phips wondered.

He prepared for a fight. But the newcomers were just two old friends of his, William Davis of Bermuda and Abram Atherley of Jamaica. They had been with him on his first voyage. Phips' license from the king would have allowed him to drive them away. But rather than fight old comrades, he took them into partnership and they joined his expedition.

The wind was fierce the next day. Captain Phips' ships tossed like corks on the water. Several times they nearly turned over. It was no calmer under the sea. Strong currents swept the divers off their feet. Most of their energy went into fighting the current instead of bringing up silver.

But the captain had brought along a diving bell for rough weather. This early model was a wooden cask, open at the bottom. When it was lowered straight down into the water, some air stayed inside it, just as a drinking glass will hold some air when put upside down into a pail of water.

The diving bell held enough air for forty-five minutes' work undersea. After much difficulty the men were able to lower it properly. It dangled fifteen feet above the wreck. Now the diver had a supply of air he could return to when his breath ran short.

The diver Franko went down. He slid between the

shattered timbers of the hull and started to attach a hook to a valuable gun that lay inside. A minute went by, a minute and a half. Still he worked furiously. His lungs were close to bursting. He thought the diving bell was just above him, but the current had swept it out of his reach. Breathless, he forced his way out of the wreck. His line caught on a timber! He freed it and was pulled to the surface. He was hauled on deck unconscious but still alive.

The divers went back to the old method of diving and coming to the surface for air.

The men worked eight or nine hours a day, making about twenty dives an hour. This went on for six weeks. On March 3, the big brass gun came to the surface, and five thousand pieces of eight. A few days later a ton of silver coins was brought up. Another ton of silver, a bar of gold, and sacks of jewels came on deck on the eighth of March.

The four bold Indian divers were showing the strain. They came up gasping now. They lay on the deck between dives, weak and dizzy. The twenty dives each hour dwindled to fifteen, then to ten, at last to five.

Time was running out. March storms tossed the ships about. At any time, pirates might attack and rob them of all their hard-won treasure. Captain Phips urged his tired divers on. There seemed to be no end to the treasure. More and more silver came from the wreck in the sea.

Finally the captain decided they could stay no longer. The divers were weary. Supplies were running low. The weather was bad.

In mid-April they called a halt to the diving. Heavy with treasure, the *James and Mary* and the *Henry* set sail.

They headed first toward the nearby Turk Islands to rest a few days. The *James and Mary* nearly ran aground there. They rested at Cotton Cay, thinking sadly of the treasure they had had to leave in the sea.

After leaving Cotton Cay, the *Henry* foundered and sank. Luckily, all the treasure was now aboard the *James and Mary* but she was alone. She was a slow, clumsy ship, and would be helpless against pirate attack.

Captain Phips kept a round-the-clock watch. He steered clear of the known shipping lanes. He did not even risk stopping at Bermuda for food. He feared pirates might be waiting for him there. So the long trip back to England was made with a half-starved crew.

As the days passed, there were complaints and whispers of mutiny among the sailors. Some of the men considered killing Captain Phips and sharing the treasure among themselves. The captain got word of the plot. He promised all the men a large bonus when they landed in England. So that and his real popularity with his men ended the plot.

On June 10, 1687, the *James and Mary* anchored in the Thames River just outside London. Word was carried to Captain Phips' old friend, the Duke of Albemarle. In the middle of the night the duke hastened eagerly to the harbor, and heard the good news from the treasure hunters themselves.

The next day all London celebrated wildly. Brawny Bill Phips, the adventurer from Maine, was the hero of England. The treasure was fabulous. Thirty-five tons of silver, plus gold and jewels and cannon. Today such a treasure would be worth five million dollars!

Captain Phips kept a quarter of a million. Twice that much went to the king. All the rest was shared by the backers and the crew. The captain was called to Windsor Castle, where the delighted James II touched his sword to Phips' shoulder and commanded him to "Arise, *Sir* William Phips!" He was now a knight.

King James offered Sir William any position he wanted. Phips chose to be the provost marshal general of the Massachusetts Bay Colony. After many months of living a hero's life in London, he returned to America, wealthy and famous and a holder of high office.

A later attempt to finish the salvage job at Ambrosia Bank did not succeed. But Sir William Phips' fame grew. He led a successful expedition against the French in Canada. Later he persuaded the new King of England, William III, to restore the original colonial charter of Massachusetts. He was appointed the first royal governor of the Massachusetts Bay Colony under the restored charter.

The fortuneteller's words had come true. In 1687, when he was thirty-seven, William Phips had found a great treasure. Four years later he was the king's governor in Massachusetts. He was a hero in his native land and in England. Without the help of today's modern treasure-finding devices, he brought fantastic wealth out of the sea.

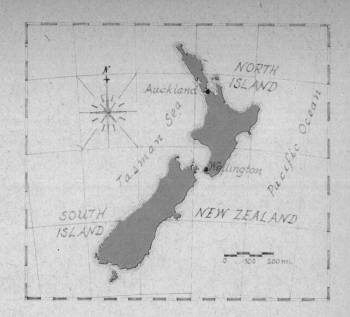

The Secret Search

Jᴜɴᴇ 19, 1940. The *Niagara,* a thirteen-thousand-ton steamer, is bound for Vancouver out of New Zealand. In the dark hours of the night, a savage explosion rips the ship apart! The cry goes out: "Away all boats! We've hit a mine! *We're going down!*"

Thirty miles from Whangarei Harbor, the *Niagara* slipped beneath the waves. The passengers and the crew, escaping without loss, rejoiced at their good luck in getting clear. But the captain of the *Niagara* was deep in gloom. Not only had his ship gone down, but it had taken to the bottom a highly secret precious cargo: ten million dollars in gold bars, bound for America to pay for war material. And the gold was not insured!

It was a terrible blow to war-torn Great Britain, for the gold was vital to England's defense. Every ounce was important. The gold *had* to be saved.

But the gold was hundreds of feet below the surface. It seemed impossible to bring it up. The British Admiralty did not think it could be done. Then the Australian naval authorities found a man willing to tackle the "hopeless" job. He was Captain J. P. Williams of Melbourne.

"We don't know it's impossible until we've tried," Captain Williams declared. "I'm eager to have a try."

The bold captain was faced with a tremendous job. No one knew how deep the *Niagara* lay, but everyone agreed it was beyond the range of a diver in a regular suit. That meant a special diving chamber would have to be built, since no diving chambers were available in wartime.

A Melbourne engineer quickly designed a chamber. It was a cylinder nine feet six inches high and weighed three tons. It could withstand crushing pressures as deep as a thousand feet beneath the surface. Seven glass windows around the top and more at eye level allowed the diver to look out.

The diver would wear a breathing mask connected to a can of soda lime. The soda lime swallowed up poisonous carbon dioxide and kept the air pure while the chamber was below the surface.

A ship was needed now. No seaworthy ships were available; all of them were tied up in the war effort. Finally Captain Williams found an ancient vessel, the *Claymore,* in Auckland harbor.

It was an old, small ship, so worn out that grass grew on her decks. But her engines still had life. Captain Williams hired the elderly steamer, had her patched into shape, and chased round the docks looking for the gear he needed for an expedition.

His mission was a secret one. The British people would have been terribly discouraged if they had known that the *Niagara* had gone down with millions of dollars in gold aboard.

December had come. On December 9, the *Claymore* headed toward the spot where the *Niagara* had sunk. Captain Williams had with him a crack crew and two ace divers, John Johnstone and his brother William.

The searchers believed that the wreck lay somewhere in an area of sixteen square miles. Marking it out with buoys, Captain Williams started dragging a sweep back and forth along the track in hopes it would tangle in the wreck.

On the second day, at four in the afternoon, the sweep caught! The *Claymore* marked the spot with a buoy. But just then a gale arose, driving the little vessel back to Whangarei Harbor before a search could be made.

There were more delays. Not until December 29 did a diver take the chamber toward the bottom, 408 feet down. But his report brought despair to the men who waited far above him on deck.

"It isn't the *Niagara*, Captain. It seems to be a rock!"

Disappointed, John Johnstone returned to the surface. But trouble presented itself. A wire caught the diving chamber on the way up. Johnstone cleared it and reached the deck, only to find that the wire had been attached to an explosive mine that now drifted only six feet off the *Claymore's* bow!

The mine was entangled in their anchor cable. A touch, a violent shock, and the *Claymore* and all hands could be blown high out of the water.

Bravely, Chief Diver Johnstone went overboard in a diving suit and struggled to free the mine from the an-

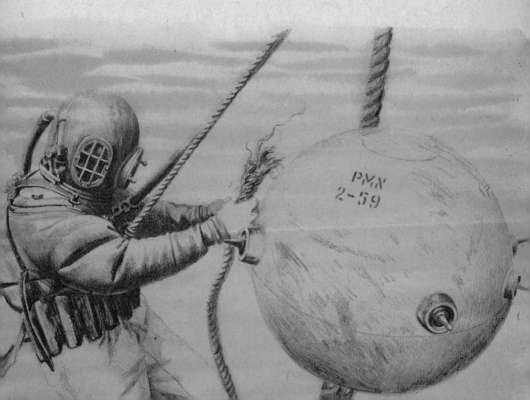

chor cable. One wrong move would mean death to all. Finally he had to be hauled out, too tired to go on.

The mine was still there.

A mine sweeper, a ship designed to get rid of mines, was called. Once again, John Johnstone went over the side — this time, to attach a line from the sweeper to the mine. The sweeper would snap the mooring, bring the mine to the surface, and explode it harmlessly.

The mine bobbed just below the waves. With great difficulty Johnstone made the line fast around the mine. In doing so, however, he became entangled with the mine. He rested on top of it, knowing it might blow up at any moment. After a while he was able to free himself, and the mine was destroyed without causing any damage. It was a terrifying interlude that nearly ended the search for the *Niagara* at its very beginning.

The sweeping of the ocean bottom continued on into January. Captain J. W. Herd joined Captain Williams to help in the job. And at ten o'clock in the morning, January 31, 1941, the *Claymore's* sweep caught fast and the little ship came to a halt.

The crew was cheerful but not very hopeful. For all they knew, it might be another false alarm.

But not this time. John Johnstone went down again in the diving chamber on February 2 and returned grinning. It was indeed the *Niagara* — at a depth of 438 feet!

The next day, Johnstone went down again to look at

the ship. Hundreds of feet above him, the little craft to which he was connected bobbed wildly on the stormy sea. He was set down, in his chamber, on the *Niagara's* deck. Suddenly the chamber was yanked up, slung across the wreck, and sent crashing into the mud at the bottom, as the *Claymore* on the surface pitched and turned.

Johnstone was hauled to the surface quickly. The unexpected jolt had left him bruised and battered, but both the sturdy diving chamber and the iron-willed diver had come through safely.

During the weeks that followed, the Johnstone brothers explored the wreck and charted it. Their task was made harder by the need to remain in the diving chamber, and by the terrific gales and bobbing mines that beset the *Claymore* on the surface. Captain Williams and Captain Herd made a cardboard model of the sunken ship to study the best way of blasting in toward the gold.

The blasting job was long and tiring. The man in the diving chamber had to keep signaling up by telephone, telling the men on deck where he wanted to be hoisted for placing the explosive charges.

"Swing me a yard to the right . . . a little bit more . . . that's it . . . just a shade up now . . . no, too much, let me down. . . ."

It was hard work, but finally a hole was blasted in

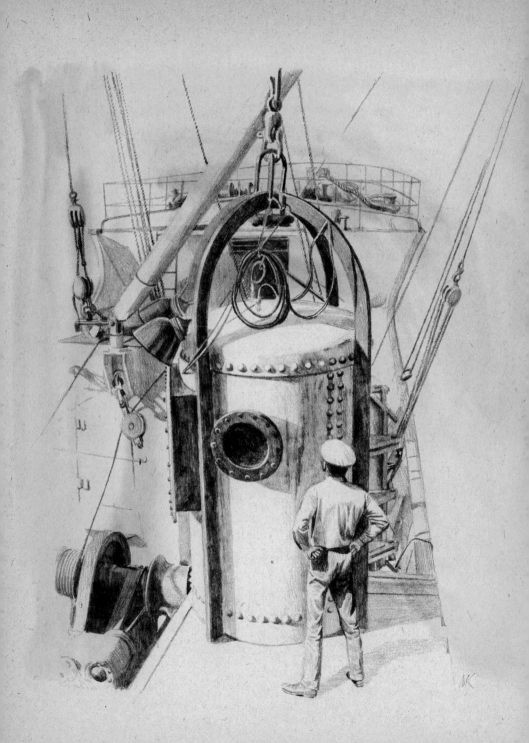

the side of the ship. A machine called a grab was sent in to haul out the debris that blocked the men from the gold. Day after day, the debris came out. Sometimes the fierce gales made work impossible. On other days, the diver could not see at all on the bottom.

"Maybe the gold isn't even in the ship," the men suggested. "Maybe it fell right through the hold and is buried forever in the mud down there."

These gloomy ideas were shouted down, and the work went on. Now there was a gaping wound sixty feet long torn in the side of the ship, down through two decks to the strong room.

A steel door blocked the last step into the strong room. The ship had tipped over on her side, and behind the door stood 590 bars of gold, weighing more than eight tons — and worth thirty-five dollars an ounce. The door too had to be blasted away. But there was the risk of blasting too hard, and scattering the precious yellow metal out into the black sea bottom, beyond all hope of recovery. The charge had to be just the right size, and it had to be placed at just the right point near the door. For hours, they worked to put the charge where they wanted it. At last, success was theirs. The door was blasted off perfectly!

The strong room now lay open. But much work still remained. Day after dreary day, the big grab stretched its metal jaws into the strong room, coming out with loads of useless rubbish that had fallen into the hole. Two weeks went by with nothing but muck and filth coming up.

October 13, 1941 — sixteen months after the sinking of the *Niagara* — the grab swung up from the depths.

"Gold! It's brought up gold!"

The first box of gold had come back from its watery grave.

The men of the *Claymore* were happy that night. And now the work went ahead with more energy than ever. The divers squinted through the portholes of the diving chamber, telephoning instructions up to Captain Williams and Captain Herd. The captains passed them along to the men operating the big winches, or hoisting machines. Down went the grab, forward into the strong room. The metal jaws snapped shut. Up came the grab — sometimes with gold, more often with mud or rubbish.

The gold began to mount up. By November 6, three and a half weeks after the finding of the treasure, more than three million dollars in gold bars was aboard the *Claymore.* On November 11 alone, a fantastic record was set as ninety-two bars — worth close to $1,500,000 — came from the bottom in only six hours!

The men worked furiously. England needed that gold to pay for the guns that would drive back Hitler's invading armies. Eighty-nine bars left the sea on November 19, forty-eight more the next day. Even the captain's cabin on the *Claymore* overflowed with gold bars.

Never in history had so much gold been recovered so fast. In five short weeks, eight million dollars in bars was brought up! The mopping-up operations now began. Most of the gold was safe, but thirty-eight bars — a king's ransom in themselves — still had escaped the grab.

The diving chamber itself went into the strong room. Diver John Johnstone peered into the dim depths and uncovered a box of gold that had escaped the grab until then. His brother William took charge of bringing it up. But one bar seemed to mock them. It was thrust in at an angle, and it seemed as if the grab could never capture it. Scores of attempts were made, all in vain, before the stubborn bar of gold at last came free!

The hunt was over.

It had taken eleven months and three weeks, altogether. The men of the *Claymore* had worked tirelessly in a region of the sea studded with deadly mines, and their triumph was complete. They had rescued eight tons of all-important gold from the kingdom of the sea in record time.

For the weary old *Claymore*, it was the last voyage. Not long after her return, the sea broke through her worn-out plates and ended her career on the seas. But she had done noble service on her final trip. And Captain Williams and Captain Herd, Divers John and William Johnstone, and all the men of the crew had the joy of knowing they had shared in one of the most amazing underwater feats in history.

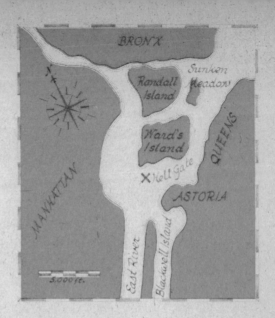

Gold in the River

THE YEAR WAS 1932. For Simon Lake it was a year of dreams — dreams of sunken gold. He stood on the Manhattan shore, staring at the section of the East River known as Hell Gate.

"There's four million dollars of George the Third's gold down there," he muttered to himself. "And I'm going to find it!"

Simon Lake was a dreamer, but some of his dreams came true. In the 1890's when submarines still seemed like science fiction, he dreamed he could build a submarine that would operate on the high seas, and he built one. It was called the *Argonaut*. On its trial run in 1897 he surprised the world by voyaging under water from

Virginia to New York. Like many inventors, Simon Lake never grew rich from his inventions. He spent every dollar he had to prove that submarines could be useful. He was right, of course, but he died a poor man.

So Simon Lake was interested in recovering gold. That, he thought, was one way a man could gain wealth quickly! If building submarines would not bring him fortune, then he would use his underwater vessels to bring up hidden treasure!

And treasure lay right in New York's own East River — the treasure of the sunken *Hussar*.

His Majesty's Ship *Hussar* was a stout, copper-plated frigate 114 feet long, with twenty-eight guns. She anchored at New York on September 13, 1780, during the Revolutionary War. There she was loaded with money to pay British troops fighting in Virginia. More than four million dollars in gold was supposed to have been stored in the frigate's hold — along with fifty American prisoners.

The *Hussar's* gold never reached the king's soldiers in Virginia. Going through the dangerous Hell Gate passage in the East River, the ship collided with Pot Rock. Water thundered through the crushed hull. The gold-ship was doomed!

Desperately, her captain ran her ashore. But the shore was rocky and the tides were high. A landing was impossible. The crew managed to scramble ashore. But down went the ship, the gold, and the helpless prisoners to the bottom, seventy-five feet below.

At once the *Hussar's* commander, Sir Charles Pole, declared that there had been no money on board. Everyone knew, though, that he was only trying to keep the gold out of the hands of the colonial army. People had seen four iron chests of gold and ten boxes of silver being carried on board the ship.

With so much gold lying right off the shore of New York City, there were many attempts to reclaim it. A man named Samuel Davis is said to have slipped cables under the *Hussar's* stern in 1823 in hopes of lifting her. But the cables parted and the wrecked ship fell back into the sea. Later, British divers went down in a diving bell, without results.

For thirty years after that, a Captain Taylor of Massachusetts worked on and off at finding the *Hussar's* treasure. He had no luck, either, although his group was the first to use the "newfangled" diving suits while trying.

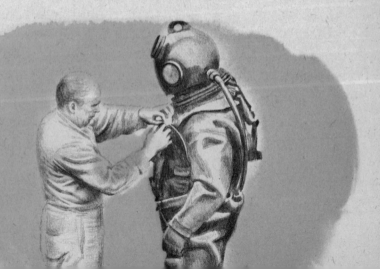

The problem was that the wreck was covered by a thick layer of silt. The treasure hunters could reach the gun deck, but they could not get into the hold. Still, the Taylor company managed to bring up a few gold pieces, proving that treasure did indeed wait in the *Hussar's* hold. Others tried, without success.

As a boy, Simon Lake stood on shore watching the steamer *Chester* pumping up East River mud in hopes of finding it rich with English gold.

"Even at this early date in my life," Simon said in 1920, "I had made plans for a salvaging submarine, and I was naturally interested in such a great treasure as the *Hussar* was supposed to have on board."

After he had built his *Argonaut*, Simon tracked down old Captain George Thomas, the man who had commanded the *Chester*.

Captain Thomas told Lake what he knew. The English had shipped the gold secretly, in fear of American spies. The money was in gold guineas, and chalk from the Dover Cliffs of England was piled over the treasure to hide it in case of capture. By the time Captain Thomas began work, he said, fifteen feet of silt covered the wreck.

For years, the *Chester* pumped mud blindly. The currents were strong, and the divers could remain on the bottom for only a short while. One diver told Lake that he had had to tie himself fast in order to work down there. In all his years of pumping, Captain Thomas had never reached the wrecked ship!

Simon Lake set about making his plans.

He formed the Lake Submarine Salvage Corporation and tried to raise $750,000 to pay for the search. But times were bad, and no banker would risk cash on such a wild-eyed scheme. Simon had to pour his own money into the project.

He got the government to give him exclusive rights to search for the *Hussar*. In return, he promised to turn over ten percent of any treasure he found, and all the cannons he brought up. In 1933, he was ready to begin.

The first and biggest problem was finding the *Hussar*. This was no simple task. The shore line had changed over the years since the sinking. Docks and a ferry slip had been built. In 1886, twenty thousand tons of rock were

dynamited out of the channel at deadly Pot Rock. Silt and mud had settled over the bottom.

But in 1903 a big anchor had been found in the river, marked *H.M.S. HUS—*. The ship could not be far away.

Simon Lake built a submarine that he called the *Laksco I*, and he gathered a small fleet of surface craft. His idea was to explore the bottom in his submarine, with all the machinery he needed riding along in a surface vessel connected with the diving ship. By 1935, he was ready to begin work.

By that time other treasure hunters had found a fifty-foot-long timber off Stony Point, near 130th Street in the Bronx. This seemed promising. Simon Lake and his crew began to explore the bottom.

But lack of money kept holding up the search. Back and forth across the river bottom Simon went, ever narrowing the area in which he expected to find the *Hussar*. To keep the money flowing, he took time off from the search for English gold to bring up coal from some of the more than fifty sunken barges in the region. But always he returned to the hunt for the *Hussar*.

He was sure he knew where it was, now. It must be off 135th Street, under twelve feet of silt and covered with a layer of tar from a nearby gas plant. But ferries unloading scrap metal were in his way. Again there were delays. Simon decided to bore into the river bottom with a core drill. If the drill brought up chalk, he would know

he had found the *Hussar*, since the English had hidden the gold under a covering of chalk.

But money was running out. Simon had poured all his funds into the search. He could not even pay the back taxes on his own home in Connecticut now! And more than a hundred drillings between 134th Street and 136th Street had yielded no chalk, no oak, nothing that would hint at the presence of the sunken treasure ship. Simon moved a little farther above 136th Street and continued drilling.

It was 1937, now. Simon Lake was seventy-one years old, blind in one eye, getting very creaky and stiff from his long years underwater. But he did not give up. "I won't stop till I'm stopped," he insisted. "My dad was ninety last Thursday. My grandfather lived to be ninety-six and his sister kept going till she was a hundred and two or so."

Simon Lake kept going, lured on by the gleam of gold. His ship found the wreck of the *Observation*, which had gone down in 1932 with about a hundred people aboard. They brought up knives, timbers, and eighty-six cents in cash.

Simon was still at it in 1939, grimly searching along the Bronx shore, turning up broken crockery, rivet heads, all sorts of worthless junk — but no gold. He begged the government to give him more time to search. "Just a little more time," he begged. "I'll find that ship!"

He had a new idea now. Perhaps the wreck had shifted into deeper waters after a clumsy attempt at lifting it over a century before. Simon remodeled his submarine *Salvager* and prepared to look farther off shore. The government told him he had just one more year to find the *Hussar*.

But World War II broke out, and Simon Lake's search was ended forever. He died in 1945, his great dream of bringing treasure from the depths still only a dream. The *Hussar's* gold still lies in the mud of Hell Gate.

Or does it? Perhaps the British claims were right, and the hull contains nothing but chalk ballast and the crumbling bones of the doomed American prisoners. Or maybe the treasure is buried forever under the foundations of the apartment houses that have been built on filled-in land.

Sturdy old Simon Lake would angrily insist that the treasure is still there for the taking. But at seventy-eight he had run out of time, never having found so much as the hull of his long-sought treasure ship.

Simon Lake's story has no happy ending. The fame rightfully due to him for his pioneer work on the submarine never came to him, and neither did the gold he sought so eagerly in Hell Gate. But his determination and courage set an example for all treasure seekers and pioneers of today. Lake was a man who would not give up. And, perhaps, if he had had a few more years, he *would* have raised the gold of King George from its watery bed.

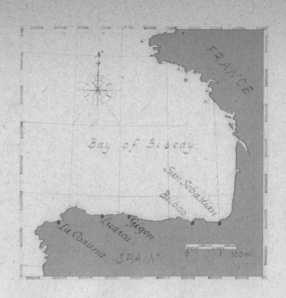

Luck and the Egypt

"Sos, sos, sos," came the feeble signal. "Position 48° 10′ N, 5° 30′ W."

It was the last message ever received from the liner *Egypt*. She had left England on May 19, 1922. Her first stop was to be the port of Marseilles, France. After that she was bound for India. But she never even got to Marseilles.

On her second day at sea, shortly after seven, another ship loomed up suddenly out of a heavy fog. It was the *Seine*, a large cargo steamer with a sturdy hull. The ships collided. The *Seine* knifed through the timbers of the old *Egypt*.

In twenty minutes the *Egypt* was four hundred feet below the surface of the Bay of Biscay. More than two hundred people went down with her. So did ten tons of silver and five tons of gold, worth more than five million dollars.

The treasure had been insured by Lloyd's of London, a famous insurance company. They paid up in full. No one would ever reclaim the lost gold, people said. After all, the *Egypt* was four hundred feet down. There had never been a successful salvage operation at such a great depth. No one had ever even brought treasure up from *two* hundred feet!

In Genoa, Italy, one man refused to listen when people said it was impossible to bring up the treasure of the *Egypt*.

"There is always a first time," said short, chubby Giovanni Quaglia, the son of a rich man. "I will salvage that gold no matter what they are saying."

Quaglia was a champion athlete, a crack rifle shot, and a successful businessman. At fifty-nine, he was wealthy and bored. He wanted adventure — the high adventure of a treasure hunt. He organized a company to salvage the *Egypt*.

The first step was to buy the rights to use a remarkable new German diving device. This made use of a tremendously strong shell of metal. The diver remained inside. The outer shell would withstand the crushing pressure of the sea, and the diver could breathe normal air inside instead of compressed air. That arrangement saved much precious time on each dive.

Seven years went by while Quaglia became an expert at underwater treasure hunting. He raised other ships, bringing up seven locomotives from one and a fortune in ivory from another.

At last, in 1929, he decided he was ready to tackle the *Egypt*.

He sailed for the French port of Brest with two ships, the *Artiglio* and the *Rostro*, and four divers, Gianni, Raffaelli, Bargellini, and Franceschi. The experts told him he was a madman to try it. At four hundred feet the underwater pressure was 177 pounds to the square inch.

Savage currents would batter the divers mercilessly. It was too dark to work down there. The task was hopeless.

Quaglia paid no attention. He set about the job of finding the sunken ship.

He and his chief diver, Alberto Gianni, studied the charts. They noted the *Egypt's* position when it went down, thirty miles off the French coast. They allowed for the currents. Finally they plotted out an area of forty square miles on the map. Somewhere in that rectangle lay the *Egypt*. If they had to, Quaglia vowed, they would search every inch!

In May 1929, they began looking. The *Artiglio* and the *Rostro* were tiny vessels. They anchored in the bay and divers went down. They found nothing. Storms forced them back to shore.

A week later they set out again. This time they dragged a steel cable two thousand yards long between the two ships in hopes of snagging it on the wreck. Soon the cable caught. Excitement rose aboard the ships! But then the cable slipped loose.

"It's a rock," diver Gianni said disgustedly.

It turned out that the bottom was studded with jagged, dangerous rocks. A new kind of sweep was invented that would not catch on rocks. They continued south.

The sweep caught again!

Gianni tried to go down to see what was there, but the sea was too rough. Instead, they dropped a buoy to mark the spot. They would come back again when the weather was better for diving.

As they tried to pull their cable loose, it broke. They hauled it in. It was marked with smears of white paint. And the *Egypt* had been painted white! Quaglia and his men cheered wildly.

For a week they waited impatiently ashore. At last the sea grew calm, and they set forth again. But a bitter disappointment was in store for them. The marker buoy had broken loose in the storm! They had no way of finding the wreck now.

Quaglia tried everything. He was financing the whole expedition out of his own pocket, and though he was wealthy his funds would not last forever. The wreck had to be found quickly.

He called a priest with a reputation in Italy for being able to find ore in the ground. The priest failed to locate the *Egypt*. Magicians offered to find him the wreck if he would give them part of the treasure. They failed.

A month went by. Still the search produced nothing. The tides and storms were fierce. The divers could work no more than four hours a day, ten days out of a month, three months out of the year. At that rate, they could hunt for years without finding the ship.

Giovanni Quaglia began to lose hope. Suppose they were right, the mockers who had told him his search was foolish!

In the summer of 1930 he tried again. Captain le Barzic, who had commanded the *Seine* when it rammed the treasure ship, joined the *Artiglio* to help in the search. They explored the region, Barzic guiding them to the place where he thought the *Egypt* had gone down. The newly invented sweep dragged up dozens of other worthless wrecks, but never the *Egypt*. They went from south to north, and back again.

Late one day the drag caught for perhaps the hundredth time. A storm was coming up, so they dropped a buoy at the spot and left. They spent an anxious night ashore, wondering if a storm would once again rob them of their prize.

No! The buoys were in place the next day, all but

one that had drifted half a mile away. The diver Gianni decided to pick up the drifting buoy before beginning the dive. They steamed alongside the runaway and tried to haul it in.

It was caught fast. The *Artiglio's* winches groaned, and then the buoy left the water. It brought with it a shaft of rusty metal from some sunken ship with which it had become entangled.

Diver Bargellini went down to look at the unexpected find. And this time luck was with the treasure hunters — wonderful luck.

"It's the *Egypt,* all right!" he reported. And so it was. That night the treasure hunters were very happy.

The next day, the divers went down. They cut their way into the weed-covered ship and brought up the captain's safe. It was empty! The treasure lay hidden still deeper, in specially built strong rooms.

It was now too late in the season to continue work. Quaglia carefully marked where the wreck lay, and the two ships left. They planned to return the following spring to bring up the gold from the bottom.

But a terrible thing happened. To give his men other work during the winter, Quaglia agreed to work on an American ship that had sunk in the harbor of St. Nazaire. Her name was the *Florence.* She was blocking harbor traffic, and Quaglia was to remove her.

There were unexploded bombs aboard the *Florence,*

but they had been under water thirteen years. Gianni and his divers were sure that by this time they were harmless. They planted new explosives to destroy the wreck. Nineteen men aboard the *Artiglio* waited to see the explosion.

There was a tremendous roar. The *Florence* had exploded, all right, but the bombs aboard her had gone off as well!

The nearby *Artiglio* was blown to splinters. Only seven men lived. Among the dead were chief diver Gianni and his skilled helpers Franceschi and Bargellini.

Quaglia was very unhappy over the loss of these brave men. But he was more determined than ever to find the *Egypt's* gold. He bought a shabby old fishing ship and called it the new *Artiglio*. He hired three new divers and put Mario Raffaelli, the only diver left of the original four, in charge of the work.

Quaglia's money was running out now. This was his third season at work on the *Egypt*, and it might have to be his last. In May 1931, the new *Artiglio* headed for the spot where the *Egypt* lay.

The treasure was at the very bottom of the boat, under four decks, in a room twenty-five feet long and five feet wide. The divers had to blast the ship apart to get down to it. Dangling on their long cables, they placed explosive charges with great care, four hundred feet below the surface.

The weather was against them. They could only work twelve days in June, five and a half in July. Once, during an eight-day stretch of perfect weather, they pierced through three decks, making a path nearly to the treasure vault.

By the end of August they had put in twenty-eight working days and had made two hundred dives. Nothing had been salvaged except some copper pipe worth eighty-seven dollars. But it seemed the end was in sight. And just in time! Quaglia had spent $400,000 of his own and had borrowed heavily as well. His funds were almost gone.

"They're betting we'll never find the gold," he told his divers. "But we'll make them lose their bets!"

Chief diver Raffaelli went down to look around. To his horror, he found that an entire steel deck still blocked them from the treasure. Instead of days, they were *weeks* away from the gold!

September became October, and Quaglia borrowed more money to pay for his search. Far into autumn the divers worked, later than ever before.

On December 1, diver Lenci actually entered the treasure room at last. But winter had closed in. The work had to stop.

All that winter, Quaglia borrowed money, insisting that the gold was within his grasp. In May 1932, the final season of work began. He would be a ruined man if no gold was found now.

The original plan had been to raise the entire strong room by steel cables attached to floats. This, though, was impossible. Divers would have to go down and bring the treasure up, bar by bar, in special scoops operated from within the massive diving suits.

It took a month before the last remaining plate was pierced. The first scoop came out of the sea, dripping, weed-laden. It opened and out tumbled — *cartridges!* Cartridges by the thousand. Then a rotted Bible, other books, spoons and forks, and three silver dollars from Malaya. Then a loaded pistol, a dictionary, silk, foreign paper money reduced to useless pulp, pieces of wood, and rubbish — but no gold.

On June 22, three weeks after scooping had begun, Quaglia reached into the latest scoopful of muck and plucked forth an English coin.

"Look!" he cried. "A gold sovereign! *Gold!*"

Diver Lenci went down with the grab again. It rose, dripping. Every man on deck held his breath. The jaws of the scoop opened — and dropped two bars of gold on the deck.

It was a great moment. Quaglia and his men bowed their heads in memory of the brave comrades they had lost two years before. Then work began again. Seventeen more gold bars, then eleven, then some silver. By that night, 254 pounds of gold were aboard.

More was coming up — $250,000 an hour. In three days, Quaglia had recovered more than the entire cost of all the long years of work.

For the rest of that summer, and for the next three summers as well, they worked at the pleasant task of hauling treasure from the sea. By the end of 1935 they

were finished, having found more than ninety per cent of the precious cargo. Even after Quaglia had paid his happy crew and had divided the treasure equally with the insurance company, he was still a rich man.

The company Giovanni Quaglia founded to bring treasure from the sea is still in existence, and it now operates five vessels. But none of its later achievements are as impressive as its first — the four-year struggle to snatch the treasure of the *Egypt* from the determined grasp of Mother Ocean.

Treasure Overboard!

At the bottom of Vigo Bay, off the northwest coast of Spain, lies one of the richest of all sunken treasures. For 250 years people have been trying to find it. How it came to be there is a strange story indeed.

It was late in the summer of 1702. England and the Netherlands were at war with Spain and France. For three years, no treasure had been shipped from Spain's rich possessions in the New World.

The Spanish had forced millions of Indians to mine gold and silver for them in South and Central America. They had let the treasure pile up there, rather than have it captured by English pirates. Now, though, it was decided to ship the treasure to Spain, in spite of the risk. No doubt the king of Spain needed war funds.

A fleet of seventeen Spanish treasure ships sailed from America under the command of Admiral Manuel de Velasco. Two dozen French warships went with the treasure fleet to protect it.

The treasure was fantastic. There were 3400 tons of gold and silver — worth hundreds of millions of dollars!

The treasure fleet was to sail to Cadiz, Spain. But the city of Cadiz was under attack by English ships. They had been driven off, but were lurking not far from the Spanish coast. The French commander suggested that the wisest thing to do was to take the treasure to some French port until the English had sailed for home.

Admiral Velasco would have no part of such a plan. "The treasure is supposed to be brought to Spain," he declared stubbornly. "And to Spain it will go!"

But how? Cadiz was under a blockade, and the treasure ships could not get through. Even worse, a new British fleet of twenty-seven ships-of-war had got word of the treasure and was sailing to head it off. Velasco was caught between two enemy fleets. He made a run for Vigo, the nearest Spanish port.

The ships dropped anchor in the bay. Safe, so the admiral thought! But now red tape ensnarled everything. The admiral naturally wanted to unload his treasure before the English could seize it, but port officials would not allow it.

Pointing to his papers, they solemnly declared, "The

treasure is bound for Cadiz. It can only be unloaded there."

Admiral Velasco raged and stormed, but nothing could be done. He was told that rules had to be followed. The consent of the king was needed to change the port of unloading, and even then many papers would have to be filled out.

For an entire month, the admiral fretted in Vigo while the foolish port officials kept the treasure from being unloaded. Finally the English came along. Twenty-five English and Dutch ships appeared in Vigo Bay. The harbor had been blocked by a floating chain of logs and cables, but the invading fleet easily smashed through it.

French Admiral Chateau-Renault struck back with every ship he had. But the invaders tore right through the defending French warships and sent seventeen of them to the bottom in two hours. The Spanish treasure fleet was trapped!

Sinking ships were everywhere in the bay. Admiral Velasco saw his defenders ablaze and going under. He gave an order that must have hurt him bitterly.

"Get rid of the treasure! Dump it overboard! Don't let the enemy get their hands on it!"

Quickly the sailors began dumping fortunes in gold and silver into the bay. But they were not quick enough. The English and Dutch were closing in.

A new order went out: *"Sink the treasure ships!"* Decks

were set afire. Spanish sailors manned the lifeboats and rowed desperately for shore as the great treasure fleet sank. By the time the invaders reached the fleet, most of the galleons were on they way down. But several were captured still afloat, and their treasure, more than $35,000,000, was taken off to England. The rest went to the bottom. It was an unhappy day for Spain.

Not all the captured treasure reached England, though. One galleon bearing half the English loot struck a rock at the mouth of Vigo Bay and sank with three hundred tons of treasure aboard. Most of what did get to England was silver. It was melted down and turned into English coins stamped with the word *VIGO* in honor of the great victory.

Uncounted millions lay beneath the sea after the battle.

The war ended before long, and the Spanish government set about to recover its sunken loot. They thought it would be easy. The wrecked ships lay in only sixty or seventy feet of water.

But the bottom of Vigo Bay oozes with mud. More is deposited there all the time. Soon the sunken ships were buried under many feet of silt and slime.

Still, the treasure seekers went to work. Nearly every year, someone tried to find the gold of Vigo Bay. The biggest excitement in those early years came in 1728, when a French salvage firm managed to get chains around one ship and drag it to shore. But to their disgust, they found they had not found a treasure ship at all. It was only one of the sunken French warships!

Twenty years later, a man named Juan Antonio Rivero recovered some 200,000 silver pieces of eight. And in 1772, an Englishman named William Evans went down with a specially designed diving bell and came up with a good deal of silver. But little else was taken from the great treasure during its first hundred years in the depths.

In 1825 a mysterious English expedition visited Vigo Bay and may have been very successful. We will never know. One of the Spanish men hired by this group complained that Spanish divers were sent down during the daytime to clear away mud and wreckage, and then in the night English divers secretly went down to collect gold and silver. After a year's work, the Englishmen left suddenly. They claimed to have found nothing — but legend says that they took millions from the bay.

During the next forty years, many treasure hunters tried their luck and found almost nothing. In 1869, a French expedition arrived with some new inventions, such as a diving bell that had electric lights. They brought up some silver plates and several cannons, but they had to give up work when the Franco-Prussian War broke out.

At the same time an American named Colonel John E. Gowen formed a company and sent down divers. Several wrecks were dynamited, but no treasure was found in the thick mud. Gowen's company gave up, but other Americans tried again in 1885. Like the English hunters of sixty years before, they claimed to have recovered nothing, but some people say that they really found a great deal.

With the turn of the century came thirty-five-year-old Jose Pino, who showed up armed with all kinds of new pumps, magnets, and diving equipment. Pino charted the location of most of the wrecks and had a good deal of luck finding treasure. His men found gold statuettes, Mexican gold coins, bars of silver weighing up to eighty pounds, cannons, anchors, and other valuable items. Pino worked on and off in Vigo Bay for twenty-five years. He enjoyed more success than any of the other seekers after gold, for he found at least four million dollars.

After Pino came a Dutchman named van Wienen. He invented a tube designed to bore through the mud to the treasure galleons. This was useful, for by now thirty to fifty feet of mud covered the ships.

Van Wienen's work was interrupted by World War II. In 1955, the Spanish government granted a three-year license to an American-owned company for work in Vigo Bay. They raised cannon balls, pottery, porcelain pieces, and other interesting treasures.

What about the gold? Is it still there?

More than two and a half centuries have passed since Admiral Velasco ordered the treasure fleet to be sunk. Today, little remains of the sunken galleons but pieces of rotted wood. But the bulk of the treasure must still be down there in the mud.

The *Monmouth's Prize,* which was the captured galleon sunk as it headed for England, had ten million dollars worth of silver aboard. The ship has never even been found. And many other treasures have escaped the searchers. For every gleaming gold doubloon brought up, dozens more lie hidden below.

Beneath a blanket of ooze and slime, Spanish doubloons wait in Vigo Bay, bars of gold and silver worth millions, glittering jewels that could ransom a king. The prize is there — a hundred million dollars or more — patiently waiting for someone to find it.

Pesos in the Sea

THE EARLY DAYS OF 1942 were dark ones for America. We were just barely beginning to get over the surprise blow dealt us at Pearl Harbor. The Japanese soldiers had poured over the islands of the Pacific. It seemed that they would sweep right across the vast ocean.

American forces under General Douglas MacArthur were trying bravely to defend the Philippine Islands. But island after island fell to the invaders. The citizens of Manila, the capital, hurried away. The Americans were driven back until all they held was the peninsula of Bataan and the small island of Corregidor.

The gold and silver reserves of the Philippine government were hidden in vaults on Corregidor. All other official funds were taken there as the retreat continued.

Millions upon millions of Philippine pesos, each one worth fifty American cents, piled up on Corregidor.

But as the days passed, it became clear to all that Corregidor, too, was doomed to fall. Hastily, the gold and some of the silver was loaded aboard a small submarine, the *Trout*, which made a safe escape to America.

Then the little band of defenders set to work at the strange task of *destroying* $120,000,000 worth of paper money!

Day after day they hurled bundles of peso notes into blazing oil fires. It was slow work. Twenty million pesos were burned this day, twenty-five million the next, and on and on. The entire national treasury was going up in smoke while the Japanese drew ever closer. But at least the money would never be spent by the enemy.

But about sixteen million pesos — all silver coins — remained. By now it was early April 1942. Bataan had fallen, and thousands of people clustered on little Corregidor. Defeat was only days away, and there was no way of shipping the silver to America as had been done with the gold.

General George Moore, commander of harbor defense on Corregidor, gave an order: "We're going to dump all that silver into the ocean, before the Japs can get it!"

Captain James Murray of the mine layer *Harrison* was given the job. He told his crew that they had been assigned to dump "something" overboard.

One night in the third week of April, the *Harrison* slipped out to sea, heading for a deep spot in the South Channel between Corregidor and Caballo Island. Dropping anchor there, they set up a small marker buoy. Then the dumping began.

They made trip after trip back to the dock to pick up the silver. There were a thousand fat, heavy silver pesos to a bag, six bags to the box, and hundreds of boxes. The men dumped the coins as close as possible to the buoy, in the deepest part of the channel.

But some nights the buoy could not be found in the darkness. Then the sailors had to guess at the right spot. Other nights, Japanese guns forced them to dump the silver before they could reach the buoy. The buoy itself was swept back and forth by the currents. And on the sixth and last night of the dumping, Japanese machine-gun fire cut the buoy loose. Now there was no marker for the graveyard of the silver.

Only three men knew the exact spot where the buoy had been. One was killed two weeks later. The second jotted the information down, but he lost it. The third

man forgot the exact figures. The silver was scattered over more than a mile of ocean bottom, and no one knew just where it was.

At the time, no one cared very much. Japanese shelling increased, and on the fifth of May, Corregidor was invaded and fell to the Japanese. The conquerors expected to find a hoard of gold, silver, and paper money. They were disappointed to learn that all of it had either been destroyed or smuggled out under their noses.

"I shall return," General MacArthur had promised when he was forced to leave the Philippines in 1942. By October 1944, he had kept that promise. Within four months the islands had been liberated from the Japanese.

The United States armed forces had dumped the silver. Now they decided to recover it. The job went to the U.S.S. *Teak*, a stocky 165-foot ship under the command of Lieutenant Byron Hollett. The *Teak* had been at work clearing wreckage from the channel.

On June 16, the ship moved into the channel. It carried diving equipment and charts of the region. They knew *about* where the silver was supposed to be. All the rest would have to be guesswork and luck.

Divers went over the side at the spot where most of the silver was thought to be. They found no pesos. For two days they covered the muddy bottom inch by inch within a two-hundred-foot circle. Nothing.

The next day, they sent down a scoop and dragged it along the bottom. Not only did they find no pesos, but the scoop broke loose and was lost! Discouraged, they moved a few hundred feet farther on and sent a diver down. This time he found a waterlogged box!

It broke open when he touched it. Within were some three hundred silver pesos. At last, a small victory!

During the next few days, several more boxes came up. They held twelve thousand pesos. But this was only twelve thousand out of sixteen *million*.

"At this speed," Lieutenant Hollett observed sadly, "it'll take twelve years to bring up the lot."

Now came a hint. It was learned that a month earlier a group of Filipinos and some American soldiers had illegally made up a treasure hunt of their own. They had found some 500,000 pesos. The Filipino who had led the search was caught, and he was made to guide the *Teak* to the spot where he had found the silver. At least he claimed it was the spot, but nothing was found there. For six days he led the men of the *Teak* on a wild-goose chase around the channel. Then rains came for several days.

On July 8 the *Teak* crew began the search once more, discarding both the charts and the untrustworthy guide. They picked out a fresh spot completely by guess and dropped a scoop. It came up full of pesos!

A diver went down. "We've really struck it this time!"

he phoned up excitedly. "I've got five boxes right here —
and about twenty more over there — and a few more in
back of me. . . ."

The boxes and bags had rotted, and the saltwater had
glued the coins together in chunks. A ten-quart pail was
sent down on a line to the diver. He filled it as fast as

he could and brought it to the surface. As he came up, another diver went down.

Day after day, pesos were found. By August 12, more than a million pesos had ben recovered. More were coming up, twenty and thirty thousand a day. Friendly sharks visited the divers and had to be driven off. The mud was a problem, and so was the weather. Sometimes the boxes had split open in being dumped and the coins were scattered widely. But more and more were being found. On October 23 alone 86,000 coins came up, despite a visit from a huge shark. The next day, the second million was passed. On November 11, 128,000 pesos reached the surface!

But now the pesos were getting harder to find. By May 1946, the daily yield was so meager that it was no longer worthwhile to go on. In a year 5,300,000 pesos had been recovered. That was one third of the total.

The Army and Navy decided they had done well enough.

On July 4 of that year, the Philippines were made independent by the United States. The new government issued licenses to anybody who wanted to search for the ten million missing pesos. A share of what was found would have to be given to the government.

Eager treasure hunters flocked to the task. Some brought up only a few hundred pesos, others as many as 300,000.

A lucky trio of Americans started looking in January 1947. For several months they searched in vain. Then, without warning, they stumbled on a two-million-dollar jackpot!

Strangely, the United States government had just announced that there were no more pesos left. It had been learned that the Japanese themselves had brought up a great many — perhaps five or six million. Between that figure and what had been found after the war, it was supposed that all the pesos were accounted for. The announcement did not reach the three Americans for a while. If it had, they would have given up the search. They never would have made their big find!

Despite the government's announcement, other men continued to search for the pesos. Finally some official figures were released. A total of 15,792,000 pesos had been dumped. The Army and Navy had located 5,383,173 of them. Others had brought up 6,492,707 more. That left nearly four million pesos unaccounted for.

How many had the Japanese taken? Nobody knew. "Only a few thousand," some said. "Six million," guessed others. Obviously, the truth was somewhere in between. The Japanese themselves had kept no records.

Then a tattered old memo came to light. It was written by an American prisoner of war who revealed that the Japanese had conducted diving operations for four months in 1942, using captured Americans as their divers.

The Japanese had recovered 373 boxes of silver, containing 2,238,000 pesos.

So now the total is known. After fifteen years of diving by experts and amateurs, 1,678,000 pesos are still in the channel mud. The search is going on right at this moment. But, as one of the divers of the *Teak* said, "They'll likely be diving for those pesos for a hundred years to come."

Unfound Treasure

THE LOST HOARDS of the pirates. . . .

The treasure of the Incas. . . .

The untold wealth of the Spanish galleons. . . .

History is full of accounts of lost treasure. Perhaps some of these treasures are only myths and legends. Or, maybe, the value of the sunken hoards has grown as the stories were repeated through the years. But it is certain that great wealth remains to be found. . . .

When the Spanish, under cruel Francisco Pizarro, conquered Peru in the sixteenth century, they found themselves masters of a country whose land overflowed with gold and precious gems. The people of Peru were known as the Incas. They were highly civilized, and they welcomed the Spanish as friends. But Pizarro and his men were very greedy. When they saw the temples ablaze with emeralds and pearls and gold, they conquered the gentle Incas and seized the Inca treasure for their own.

The noble Inca Emperor Atahualpa was taken prisoner by Pizarro. He had to bargain for his life. Standing in a room twenty feet in length and eighteen feet wide, he said, "I will cover the floor of this room with gold if you will free me."

The Spanish could hardly believe their ears. When they did not reply at once, Atahualpa raised his offer.

"I fill the room with gold to this height," he declared.

He stood on tiptoe and touched his hand to the wall. "And I will provide twice the amount of silver as of gold."

Pizarro promised to release Atahualpa when the room was filled completely with gold to a height of seven feet. Word went out all over Peru that gold was needed to ransom the emperor. And gold began to flow toward the Spanish camp.

Day by day messengers staggered in under great weights of the yellow metal. Statues, dishes, cups, temple altars, plates of gold began to fill the room.

But the impatient Spanish grew restless. Although the gold was coming in very fast, they were not satisfied. They feared that perhaps Inca troops were gathering to attack them. There were only a few hundred Spaniards against an entire nation of Incas.

They decided to take the gold already received and move on to other territory without waiting for the full ransom to be paid. They melted down the gold they had received — twenty million dollars' worth — and they got ready to leave. They did not want to take the captive emperor with them, and so they put him to death.

The wicked act cost Pizarro and his men great wealth. For even as the sentence was being carried out, vast treasure was on its way to complete the emperor's ransom. Carriers were bringing gold by the ton. One band carried a 700-foot-long chain of gold that weighed several tons and was worth more than ten million dollars.

An endless train of llamas was trudging across the mountains, bearing seven thousand loads of gold weighing seventy-five pounds each.

None of this loot reached the Spaniards. When news came that Atahualpa had been murdered, the treasure carriers changed their direction. No one knows where they went. Some say the treasure lies buried in the jungles of Peru. Others insist that the vast hoard was hurled into the Pacific Ocean. The value of the emperor's ransom was perhaps *half a billion dollars*. For four centuries, treasure hunters have searched for the hidden wealth. But it has never been found.

The list of lost treasures is a long one. The treasure of the pirate Henry Morgan lies somewhere in the Caribbean Sea, no one knows where. And Sir Francis Drake, in 1578, threw forty-five tons of silver into the sea off Ecuador to lighten his ship. Little of that has been recovered. Off Ramsgate, England, lies the *Pereira,* proud payship of the Spanish Armada, which went down with sixteen million dollars' worth of King Philip's gold aboard. The *Debraak,* lost in the Atlantic in 1798, took fifteen million dollars with it. A mere $100,000 of this was washed up on nearby beaches; the rest remains on the ocean bottom.

The list could go on for pages. Not one of the seven seas lacks its glittering millions, its rotting galleons heavy with treasure. Perhaps someone only a boy today will be the one to recover the treasure of the *Telemaque* — twenty million dollars' worth of diamonds and rubies and gold sunk during the French Revolution. Some future explorer may find the crown jewels of Mexico's Emperor Maximilian, which went down in 1911 off the coast of Virginia.

The treasure is there. So long as gold has value to human beings, men will seek it. And find it.

Who knows?

Perhaps you will be among them.